Good Behavior Guide

Baby Tips™

The Little Terror

Other books in the Baby Tips™ series
by Charlotte Preston and Trevor Dunton

The Little Terror: Good Sleeping Guide
The Little Terror: Good Feeding Guide
The Little Terror: First Six Weeks

Good Behavior Guide

Baby Tips™
The Little Terror

CHARLOTTE PRESTON, RN TREVOR DUNTON

FISHER
BOOKS™

∾ For Alfie, Sophie, Tilly, Theo, Emilio and Sofia ∾

Publishers: Howard W. Fisher, Helen V. Fisher

North American Editor: Sarah Trotta

Book Production: Randy Schultz

Illustrations: Trevor Dunton

Cover Design: Randy Schultz

Published by Fisher Books, LLC
5225 W. Massingale Road
Tucson, Arizona 85743
(520) 744-6110

Printed in U.S.A.
Printing 5 4 3 2 1

Library of Congress Cataloging-in-Publication Data

Preston, Charlotte, 1935-
   The little terror: good behavior guide / Charlotte
Preston, Trevor Dunton. — North American ed.
      p. cm. — (Baby Tips for new moms and dads)
   ISBN 1-55561-202-4
   1. Discipline of children. 2. Parenting 3. Parent and
infant.
   I. Dunton, Trevor. II. Title. III. Title: Good behavior
guide. IV. Series.
HQ770.4.P74 1999
649'.64—dc21   99-38812
                                                                  CIP

First published in Great Britain in 1998 by Metro Books, an imprint of Metro Publishing Limited,
19 Gerrard Street, London W1V 7LA

North American edition © 1999 Fisher Books, LLC
Text © 1998, 1999 Charlotte Preston and Trevor Dunton
Illustrations © 1998, 1999 Trevor Dunton

All rights reserved. No part of this publication may be reproduced or transmitted in any form or by any means, electronic or mechanical, including photocopying, recording or any information storage or retrieval system, without written permission from the publisher, except by a reviewer, who may quote brief passages.

Notice: The information in this book is true and complete to the best of our knowledge. It is offered with no guarantees on the part of the authors or Fisher Books. Authors and publisher disclaim all liability with use of this book.

An extra note for parents with girls:

You'll find that throughout the Little Terror books we refer to babies as "he."
Please don't think we've neglected your daughters! It's purely in the interests of clarity and space.
Using he/she, him/her, himself/herself is cumbersome to read and uses valuable space that we wanted to devote to more useful topics. So, please read "she" for "he."

CONTENTS

BWAAA

This book is about helping you work with your Little Terror (LT) to create a happy, loving home. You'll learn what to expect and how to respond. The advice is practical, down-to-earth and encouraging. The suggestions should give you the confidence to deal with any problems that come up.

Having a child is kind of like being hit on the head by a falling elephant . . . nothing in life can prepare you for it. Your relationship with Little Terror can, of course, bring wonderful rewards, but you can be sure there will also be challenging moments!

TEACHING GOOD BEHAVIOR

Bad behavior or curiosity?

Children are born scientists, always experimenting and learning about the world they live in. This book will give you pointers on how to encourage this healthy curiosity by learning to tell the difference between a child's willful bad behavior and times when he's simply trying things out and testing boundaries.

What is good behavior?

Your idea of "good" or "bad" behavior is not necessarily the same as someone else's—even your partner's. Some people might go nuts when LT makes a mess. Others might see it as creativity. If one parent was brought up in a strict household and the other in a more laid-back one, they may often disagree about how LT should behave. As you'll see later in the Fair Rules section, you and your partner should reach a consensus as early as possible to give LT a clear idea of where the boundaries are.

Try to iron out your differences in advance

Some important things to remember:

① All babies and children (like their parents) are little terrors some of the time. It's part of growing up.

② All parents worry about discipline and whether they're "getting it right."

What makes a difference?

As long as LT is healthy and your expectations are realistic, his behavior, good or bad, will depend on two things . . .

Nature: Every child is born with a unique personality. This affects the way he reacts to the world and makes him who he is. Second-time parents are often amazed at just how different their new baby is from the first one.

Environment: All babies and children learn behavior from their surroundings and experiences. This means that the way you react to Little Terror has an important effect on his behavior.

The four basic ingredients for a happy child:

1️⃣ Love

2️⃣ Safety

3️⃣ Fair rules

4️⃣ Healthful diet

Whatever your situation and LT's temperament, if you can provide these four things, you'll be giving him every opportunity to grow into a strong, happy, healthy child.

Love

Love is the most important part of learning. In the beginning, crying is LT's only way of communicating with you. If he's wet, hungry or miserable, that's all he can do. If you respond to him quickly and snuggle with him, he'll feel secure, knowing that his needs will be met, that you're listening and he's loved.

Love builds LT's confidence and self-esteem. He learns by watching and imitating you. He absorbs everything that's going on around him. Even as a newborn baby he can imitate you: For example, when you stick out your tongue, he might stick out his. So if you are loving, he'll learn how to love. If you shout, he'll shout. He thinks you're the greatest and wants to be just like you. He also needs your approval—so give him lots of hugs and don't pressure him with too many expectations.

Safety

When LT starts playing on his own, cover or remove potential dangers in the room. These include open sockets, wires or cables, sharp-edged furniture, glass and any small items that are breakable or that he could put into his mouth.

Fair rules

Fair rules are about letting LT know what you can expect from each other. Think about discipline as soon as possible so you can start out the same way you wish to continue.

LT will understand rules more easily if his caregivers work as a team. Try to be consistent and strike a balance:

too strict and he might become inhibited, uncooperative, or scared to try things on his own; too laid-back and he might get out of control.

How to put fair rules into practice

Below are ten examples of fair rules about candy and other treats:

☆ Be consistent.

Don't buy him treats every time you go to the grocery store, then say no when Grandma comes with you.

☆ Be reasonable.

Don't put candy on a table near a 3-year-old and then expect him not to want it.

☆ Mean it (1).

Avoid unrealistic, absolute statements, such as, "You'll never have another treat again if you are bad," or "I'll tell your Mom when she comes home, and she'll take candy away from you forever."

☆ Mean it (2).

If you say only one treat, don't give more because he bugs you for more. This teaches him to disobey.

☆ Be understanding and loving.

If you've told him no candy and he eats some you've accidentally left lying around, let him know that you realize it must have been too hard to resist, and give him a hug. He'll learn a lot if you admit you made a mistake.

☆ **Give clear, simple instructions.**

"You can have a cookie after you eat all of your lunch."

☆ **Don't nag; he'll stop listening.**

"I've told you a million times, no more treats if you keep whining."

☆ **Don't criticize him to others, in front of him.**

"He's impossible. He never stops eating candy."

☆ **Respect his point of view and involve him in decisions.**

"What do you think about lots of treats on Saturdays, and none the rest of the week?"

☆ Punishment should be immediate and in proportion, then forgotten. Show LT he's still loved.

"You took Grandma's box of chocolates and ate them all. No sweets for you for a week and you'll have to buy Grandma another box out of your own money. Say you are sorry to Grandma." (See page 122 on discipline.)

Of course, most fair rules are common sense. It will take patience and understanding to get the balance right.

Give yourselves a break

Get a baby-sitter
and go out together,
mom and dad.
Remember, you had
a life before LT! If
you're happy, he'll
be happy.

Healthful diet

A healthful diet is crucial to LT's development, and it doesn't have to be expensive or complicated. For advice about diet, please refer to our book, *The Good Feeding Guide.*

This book covers eating behavior, good eating habits, enjoying mealtimes and developing a healthy attitude about food.

PLAY

Play is an exceptional time when LT can have fun, practice his new skills and try out your fair rules. Unless they are sick or unhappy, all children love to play. Try to anticipate LT's changing needs so

Play

the toys and activities you give him are right for his age and stage of development. Time spent playing with LT is an investment in him and is never a waste. At first, you will need to show LT how to play with things, but he'll also want to experiment and make discoveries for himself.

You don't need to play with him all the time: You can clean or cook while he plays, but always show you're interested and comment on what he's doing.

Playtime tips

Curiosity—When he's a baby and a toddler, LT will want to explore anything and everything. If he has no concept of danger or right and wrong, surprising things are bound to happen. So, when he fills your CD

player with water, count to ten and try to remember that curiosity is his way of learning about the world. Fair rules (see page 18) can help. If you use them from the beginning and teach LT what is OK with you, you'll be able to explain to him what he's done wrong without making a big deal about it.

Praise and encourage LT when he's playing nicely, and try to ignore him when he's being a pain.

Find some friends for LT to play with so he learns to get along with others. This will build confidence for when he goes to school or daycare later on.

Make play interesting. Show him things to do, look at and think about.

Encourage him to be active. When he's a baby, he'll enjoy relaxing with his diaper off. When he grows into a toddler, take him to let off steam in the park, where he can jump, climb and run around like crazy.

Let him lead. It's easy to get into the habit of telling LT what to do. Spend some time every day doing what *he* wants to do, how *he* wants to do it. It may seem weird at first, but stick with it and you'll both have a great time. You can use this kind of play to change behavior patterns, if you're having problems (see page 116).

Let LT take
the lead

Good Behavior Guide

POTTY TRAINING

It might seem like he'll never get the hang of it, but he will—when he's ready! Don't let your family and friends pressure you into starting too early and don't believe Ms. Knowitall when she tells you her nephew was potty-trained by his first birthday.

LT's nervous system won't be developed enough to know when he wants to go until he's 18 months to 2 years old. By the time he's 2, only half of his friends will be dry during the day, but by age 3, 9 out of 10 will be dry most days and 6 or 7 of them will be dry at night too. With luck, LT will be one of the early ones, but if he isn't, don't worry—by 5 years most children are dry day and night.

Potty training is an important milestone and you can help LT make the move from diapers by being relaxed about it, consistent in the training, and by giving him lots of praise. Peeing in the potty almost always happens first. Pooping comes later. Start when LT has been dry for about 2 hours, or when he has given you some big hints that he's feeling ready to start:

☆ He will start to notice when his diaper is dirty.

☆ He'll know when he's peeing, and will often tell you.

☆ He'll begin to tell you when he's about to pee.

He'll start telling you when he wants to go

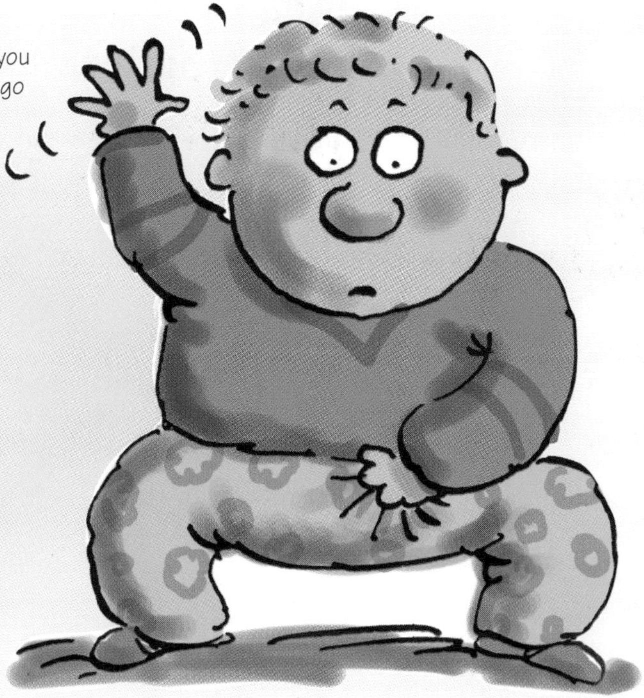

Potty-training tips

☆ **Show LT the potty.** Tell him what it's for and leave it around the house. Let him try a child's potty seat. Let him see you using the toilet.

☆ **If he poops at the same time each day,** take off his diaper and let him try the potty. If he doesn't like it, put the diaper back on and don't try again for a week or two. Give him lots of praise for performing or just for sitting there. (You don't have to reward him—if he's ready, he'll want to use the potty.)

☆ **Get LT to sit on the potty at regular times**—such as after meals and drinks, before and after his bath, first thing in the morning and last thing at night.

☆ **Leave off the diaper.** You can use training pants or have lots of extra clothes on hand, and buy some absorbent sheets for the bed in case of accidents.

☆ **If possible, start in the summer.** LT will be wearing fewer clothes, and he can run around outside without pants.

☆ **Carry backups**—a diaper and a set of clothes in case of accidents.

☆ **Accidents will happen,** so stay calm and don't show your irritation. He isn't doing it on purpose!

It may seem to take forever, but stick with it and don't worry about other kids getting there first. Remember that if there are changes or a problem at home, he may not want to use the potty for a while. Learning to use the potty will give LT a real sense of achievement.

Good Behavior Guide

Potty-training problems

If LT seems reluctant to get out of diapers, there could be several reasons. He might be slow to train because he's racing around so much he doesn't have time to sit. Try encouraging boys to pee while you hold the potty.

If he simply refuses to use the potty, talk to your healthcare practitioner. Potty training can become a battleground between LT and his parents, and refusing to train may be a symptom of deeper behavioral problems.

If he's over 5 and still wets during the day or night, ask your pediatrician to refer you to a specialist.

Tips for the reluctant sitter

☆ **Make sure he's not constipated.** It might be hurting him (try extra water and fruit).

☆ **Give him a break.** Try again in a few weeks.

☆ **Make the bathroom interesting!** Put posters and pictures on the walls. Put a special box of books on the floor next to his potty.

GOOD SLEEPING HABITS

Getting LT to develop good sleeping habits while he's still a baby will help him sleep soundly and help you return to your normal sleeping patterns sooner.

For more detailed advice, see *The Good Sleeping Guide*

zzZZZ

The aim is:

1) to start LT off with good sleeping habits, or

2) to make changes so that he learns to go to sleep and stay asleep when you want him to. He obviously won't sleep through the night at first because he'll wake up

often to eat. By about 6 months, however, he won't need so many night feedings because he'll be eating solids during the day.

The secret is to teach LT right away how to go to sleep on his own. Then, when he wakes up, he'll be able to go back to sleep by himself. Try to cut down on the times you let him fall asleep on the breast, bottle or in your arms.

Once a day, encourage LT to get himself to sleep by putting him down awake in his crib or taking him for a walk in his stroller. Try singing or gently patting him to help him settle down.

If LT doesn't fall asleep by himself right away, don't worry! LT might take a week or two to fall asleep on his own, but it will be satisfying when he does. Then try it twice a day, and so on.

With luck, by the time he's 6 months old, he'll calm down quickly during the day and go out like a light at bedtime.

Tips for the reluctant sleeper

Some babies are more reluctant than others to fall asleep on their own.

☆ **Check first for clear reasons why LT isn't falling asleep.** Is he too hot or too cold, sick, hungry or thirsty, or have there been any changes at home (a holiday, for instance)?

☆ **It's easier to teach LT how to fall asleep during the day, when you're less tired.** The best time for naps is between 9:30 a.m. and 3:30 p.m.—not too close to his usual bedtime. Regular naps won't affect how he sleeps at night.

☆ **Stay with him until he's asleep.** Try the soothing methods on page 62. He may take as long as an hour to fall asleep.

☆ **After he's used to falling asleep—**
instead of patting and singing, sit next to the crib with just your hand on him. Stay until he's asleep. After a week, start moving your chair away, about one foot every three days, until you are near the door.

When he's settling down in his crib, with you on the chair by the door, start leaving the room for ten seconds at a time. Gradually increase the time you are out of the room. It might take two or three weeks for this to work.

☆ **Establish a bedtime routine.** For example, have a quiet half-hour after bathtime, then give him a bottle or breastfeed him in the bedroom and look at a book together. Finally, snuggle with him, kiss him goodnight and leave. Use the same routine when he's older and using a bed, but instead of a bottle, use that time for brushing his teeth.

☆ When LT is about 6 months—

Gradually water down the milk in his nighttime bottle. If you breastfeed, begin feeding him fewer times each night. Pick a time when he usually eats a lot,

Good Behavior Guide

say 11:30 p.m. For three nights, try not feeding him after that until 2:00 a.m. For the *next* three nights, try not feeding him again until 2:30 a.m. Increase the time by about a half-hour every three days.

☆ **Avoid letting him sleep in your bed.**
He could overheat, which increases the risk of sudden infant death syndrome (SIDS). Once you let him sleep with you a few times, he'll think it's his right and won't be too happy if you take that right away.

☆ **If LT is sick or teething, or his routine changes,** he'll need a lot more snuggling and you won't be too successful with the tips above. Try again when he's better!

☆ **Get all the rest you can.** Ask family and friends to help you.

☆ **For more advice,** Read *The Good Sleeping Guide*, in the Baby Tips™ series.

Good Sleeping Habits

MEALTIMES

LT's mealtimes can be lots of fun. There's nothing like eating together to make you feel like a family.

All families have their own mealtime routines and yours will be different from The Knowitalls' and the Doneitalls'. LT will be learning from your behavior. If you lick your plate, so will he. Set a good example—when he begins weaning, sit down and eat or drink something with him.

Mealtimes

Most children under 5 go through stages of refusing to eat certain foods. This is perfectly normal and doesn't mean that LT will starve. If the stage lasts only a little while, he won't harm himself at all. Follow the tips on the next pages to establish enjoyable family mealtimes.

Mealtime tips

☆ **Make it fun.** Talk to LT about what you're doing.

☆ **Stick to regular mealtimes, even when he's weaning.** Don't let him pick at his food and snack.

Stick to regular mealtimes

☆ **Be prepared.** Buy groceries ahead of time and start preparing meals early so he doesn't get too hungry waiting.

☆ **Don't make eating in front of the TV a habit.** It's OK as an occasional weekend treat, but if you do it regularly, it will distract him from his meal.

☆ **Never force LT to eat.** Even when he's weaning, you'll know when he's had enough. He'll turn his head away, push his bowl on the floor, spit out his food and make some "I've had enough" noises.

☆ **Don't reward him for refusing your nutritious meal by offering him his favorite snacks.** If he hates the food you've prepared, offer him a healthful alternative.

☆ **Try to keep your cool.** It won't always be easy!

Eating problems

Most parents who worry about under-eating have babies who are well-fed or even overweight! If you stay calm and respond sensitively when LT refuses food, it probably won't become a serious problem. If he regularly won't eat anything at all, he might have found a way to get your undivided attention. Nevertheless, if you are worried, consult your healthcare practitioner, if only to put your mind at ease.

Some feeding dos and don'ts for problem eaters

DO

Encourage him to finish his meal, even if he takes forever. Try to stay calm.

Put very little on his plate to start with.

DON'T

Don't force him to eat.

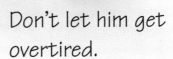

Don't let him get overtired.

DO

Give lots of praise for even a little improvement.

Eat with him, talk to him, make it fun.

DON'T

Don't give him only what you would like him to eat (be realistic).

Don't give him snacks between meals.

Good Feeding Guide

DO

Ask his friend over for lunch—the one who eats like a horse.

Invite other people to lunch; it will take the focus off LT, and you'll have a social life.

DON'T

Don't try to bribe him to eat with treats (he'll have you wrapped around his little finger and will eat nothing else).

Good Behavior Guide

WHEN THINGS GO WRONG

It's the nightmare scenario: You're at the end of your rope, LT's unhappy and behaving like a monster. How did it come to this? Things can go wrong for many reasons. Somewhere along the line, LT has learned that he gets more attention for being bad than for being good. So naturally that's what he does. The key is to change your reaction to him so that he learns he has to change his behavior.

Babies aren't born bad and parents usually do the best they can, but if LT learns he can get what he wants by acting up, he'll continue doing it.

He knows he's being naughty. Believe it or not, he still wants to please you. He doesn't really want you to be angry. He just wants your attention.

However exasperated you feel, try to talk to him and really listen to what he has to say. He'll love the attention and it may avoid the need for a confrontation.

Read through the Survival Tips for difficult behavior on page 106. Although the causes may differ, the solutions are usually the same. Also, reread the section on fair rules (page 18).

Temper tantrums

What are they? They are a violent expression of LT's frustrations and usually involve screaming, shouting, lying on the floor and crying. He might even bang his head, kick and push others, or throw things. He's unlikely to hurt himself.

BWAAA

Why *do they happen?* LT wants to do so much and can become frustrated by his immature skills. He wants to tell you things but can't get the words out (if speech development is late, this will be even harder). Maybe you were distracted when he was struggling to explain something particularly important. Perhaps he knocked over his building-block tower by mistake because he was having a bad hand-eye-coordination day. He may be jealous of a new baby and wants more love and attention. If Mom is busy, he learns that a tantrum will get him what he wants—attention. To him, any response is better than nothing.

At what age do tantrums happen? They can start before he's 18 months and peak at the terrible twos. One-fifth of parents of 2-year-olds will get a double dose each day. By the age of 4, thankfully, tantrums are rare.

When do they happen? Often when LT is tired or hungry. We've all witnessed screaming, purple-faced LTs embarrassing their parents in the grocery-store checkout line. For you as a parent, this is a no-win situation. If you reason with him, you're seen as too soft. If you get angry, you can almost hear people thinking, "No wonder the kid behaves like that." Either way, the tantrum continues. For help in situations like these, look through the Survival Tips on page 106. They might save your sanity!

You might not know exactly why a tantrum occurs, but there's no mistaking the fact LT is VERY ANGRY. Put yourself in his shoes and remind yourself how you feel when you're angry. Are you reasonable or easily pacified when you're seeing red?

LT's friends will probably range from the quiet-as-a-mouse types to raging hurricanes. At 3 years old, one child in 10 will be hyperactive and difficult to manage.

If LT is one of these, you'll need all the help you can get. He may have been born this way, sleeping little yet full of energy, zooming around, climbing over sofas, leaving the faucets running and in general getting into trouble.

An active child doesn't behave badly on purpose. He just can't contain his energy.

If this strikes terror in your heart, remember that having a lot of energy can be a big advantage in life. Here are some things you can do to help him gain more control over his life and help you rescue yours.

SURVIVAL TIPS

Tantrums?
Disobedience?
Hyperactivity?
Whatever the cause
of LT's problems, the
solutions are
generally the same.

☆ **Don't ask for trouble.** Don't go shopping when you're both irritable; it's a recipe for disaster. Plan your trip when he's not tired or hungry, and you are feeling OK. Make several short trips rather than one long one.

☆ **Provide distraction.** The best way to stop a tantrum is to catch it before it picks up speed. Build up your own set of distraction techniques. Point to something and exaggerate your interest: "Look at that bird on the tree!" or "Look! What a cute little worm." You'll sound silly, but if it works (and often it does!), who cares?

☆ **Be consistent in your own responses to LT.** If you're not, you will confuse him and he'll feel insecure. He'll also learn to take advantage.

✩ **Stay cool.** Try not to lose your temper or take tantrums personally. Shouting only prolongs the agony. The best response is to ignore a tantrum and either quietly do something else or leave the room if you can. A confrontation only makes things worse.

☆ **Don't give in.** "No" must mean "no." Don't bribe him with cuddling or treats— this teaches him that tantrums pay.

☆ **More upset than angry?** Try holding him firmly, if you are not feeling angry yourself and can reassure him.

☆ **Praise the *good things* he does** and limit the "nos" and "don'ts."

☆ **Teach him to concentrate.** Help him start playing a game and encourage him to finish it by himself with you nearby.

☆ **Make eye contact when you talk to him.** Keep instructions brief and make sure he's listening.

☆ **Take care of yourselves.** Take a break, Mom and Dad, even for just an hour or two. Ask family or friends to help.

☆ **Snuggle with him as soon as his mood improves, and drop the subject.** He's probably still upset and needs reassurance that you still love him.

☆ **Use punishment as a last resort.** *See the Discipline section (page 122) and the Time Out section (page 124).*

☆ **Be aware of the cycle of bad behavior.** *See pages 114-115.*

Cycle of bad behavior

Where does it happen?

For example, grocery-store checkout

Result

He gets what he wants.
He is in control.

Good Behavior Guide

What does LT do?

Screams for candy

What do you do?

Give him candy to keep him quiet

When Things Go Wrong

Making changes with "special playtimes"

If things are going wrong, you'll both need to make changes to improve the situation. To start with, if things are really bad, you may have to teach LT how to play. One way is to give him back a sense of control by having a "special playtime." This is a time when LT chooses exactly what he wants to do and you join in. Try starting with just 5 minutes of special playtime every day. This gives you both a chance to make real progress in your relationship. LT will feel special when you focus all your attention on him. Be realistic, though, and don't expect instant results. It will take a week or two before you both start learning how to react differently to each other.

Tips for special playtime

☆ **Let LT choose what he wants to play.**

☆ **Ask him what he wants you to do.** He might not tell you the first few times, so just watch him and give him encouragement.

☆ **Join in with LT's game.**

Good Behavior Guide

☆ **Repeat what he's saying.** For example, if LT says "I like my dinosaur," show that you've listened: "You really like your dinosaur, don't you?"

☆ **Smile and look at LT.** Give him a friendly touch or even cuddle with him if it doesn't interrupt the game.

☆ **Ignore bad behavior.**

☆ **Show LT you are interested by commenting.** For example, "You're building a big tower," or "Oh look, teddy bear's flying!"

☆ **Comment on LT's expressions.** For example, "You look happy today."

☆ **Don't tell him what to do or ask questions.** Don't try to teach him, criticize him or say no to his suggestions.

☆ **Don't interrupt or try to take control.** You want LT to enjoy himself, so give lots of praise, like "You are so smart!" or "Great job! You have built a really tall tower."

Discipline

Discipline is the last resort after you have tried everything else, LT is still acting up and you feel he's trying to make your life hell. Of course you still love him to pieces (even though sometimes it may not feel like it), but you also know you need to regain control.

You may be tempted to shout at or even spank LT, but this would actually make matters worse. He would follow your example and do the same. The first thing to do is take away the object of his bad behavior. If he's throwing toys around, remove them, or if he's kicking the TV, turn it off.

Time out

If you've tried everything else to no avail, introduce the "Time Out" technique. To illustrate this, let's use the example of LT kicking the TV.

First, tell LT not to kick the TV. If he stops, praise him and leave it at that.

If he goes right back to kick the TV, tell him you will count to 5 and if he does not obey, he'll have to sit in the hall in the "Time Out" chair. (Explain this to him as soon as you're sure he understands, so he'll comprehend when the situation arises.)

If he continues to kick the TV, tell him that he's going to the chair because he didn't do what you asked him to do.

If he goes to the chair, praise him; if not, take him to the "Time Out" chair. Make him stay there for at least 30 seconds and up to 2 minutes.

Tell LT he can leave the "Time Out" chair if he does not kick the TV. If he agrees, praise him for doing what you asked and give him a hug.

If he does not agree, repeat "Time Out" in the same way.

If he wants to stay in the "Time Out" chair for any length of time, it's not working. He may be

Make it his decision

using it to get your attention, which is rewarding him instead of punishing him. Try a special playtime (page 116) before trying "Time Out" again.

Not many parents need to go this far, but as a final attempt to change a pattern of bad behavior, "Time Out" can be effective.

By working with LT you'll understand that good behavior doesn't mean being good all the time. It's not about sitting quietly in a sailor suit, but about playing creatively and getting along with others. It's about having fun within the boundaries and sometimes testing them. All children act up sometimes, and good for them! We all need some spirit in this life.

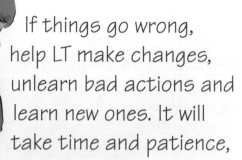

If things go wrong, help LT make changes, unlearn bad actions and learn new ones. It will take time and patience, but after a few weeks, you should notice a clear improvement in LT's behavior and in your relationship with him. If you still can't cope, your healthcare practitioner should be able to give you support or refer you to a behavioral clinic. *Good luck!*

INDEX